The
Beaver

The
Beaver

Hope Ryden

G. P. Putnam's Sons
New York

10629

Library of Congress Cataloging-in-Publication Data
Ryden, Hope.
The beaver.
Includes index.
Summary: Text and photographs describe the physical
characteristics and habits of the beaver and illustrate
the beneficial effects of his work on the environment
that he inhabits.
1. Beavers—Juvenile literature [1. Beavers] I. Title.
QL737.R632R93   1986   599.32'32   86-9425
ISBN 0-399-21364-3

This book is dedicated to
John, Dan, Nina, Henry and Tony,
who came to the aid of
a beaver colony in trouble.

Acknowledgments

I am grateful to New York state park superintendent Ken Kreisler for granting me a special permit to make nighttime beaver observations in Bear Mountain and Harriman state parks. I also wish to thank John Mead, curator of the Palisades Park Trailside Museum, for sharing with me his many firsthand observations of beaver behavior and for introducing me to an orphan kit. Without help from Joseph S. Larson, professor of forestry and wildlife management at the University of Massachusetts, I should have had great difficulty collecting current research on beaver behavior, and I am indebted to him for the use of his extensive files on the subject. Writer-naturalist John W. Miller was also of great help to me and frequently brought his sharp eyes to my study pond. Finally, I wish to thank Hope and Cavit Buyukmihci for their hospitality at Unexpected Wildlife Refuge in the New Jersey Pine Barrens, which lands they have acquired for the protection of beavers and associated wildlife. I also am grateful to Hope for her tireless efforts to educate the public on the importance of beavers through her organization, The Beaver Defenders.

H. R.

To watch a beaver work, you wouldn't suspect he could accomplish so much. He doesn't appear to be making a great effort. He may float about on the water for a time, as if thinking about what to do next, then suddenly perform a bottoms-up dive and vanish from sight. When he surfaces again, often after many minutes, he is likely to be several yards from where he went under and clasping a big wad of mud between his short front legs and fat chin. Perhaps he will use this material to stop up a break in his dam, or maybe he will plaster his big stick house with it. Whatever this beaver is up to, you are not likely to see him do it in a hurry.

Nevertheless, if you look around, you can't help but marvel at the astonishing amount of work he has managed to accomplish. Where once were fields and woods, these features have been flooded. A series of terraced ponds, each one higher than the last and each one shored up by a beautifully engineered dam, are now serving a variety of wild birds and

animals. Deer and fox come here to drink. Cedar waxwings and kingbirds flit about in the air space above the ponds, catching untold numbers of mosquitoes and other insects that hatch on the water's surface. Bullfrogs sing "jug-a-rum" to the banjo strums of common green frogs. Painted turtles sun themselves on the dam's muddy crest. Otters porpoise about and catch the fish that spawn in the watery world created by the beaver. And even in the pond's marshy inlets, ducklings paddle in their mother's wake, and muskrats weave grass houses from the stems of cattails and other reeds.

10

Cedar waxwing

Green frog

Otters

But to watch a beaver work, you wouldn't suspect so many wild creatures are dependent on him to create and maintain a home for them. Even the beaver has no inkling that his labor is so important. He works solely for himself and thus proceeds at his own, often leisurely pace, unburdened by outside pressures. One tree at a time, he fells and sections. One load of mud at a time, he scoops from the pond bottom. One stick at a time, he adds to his dam.

And after he has done a certain amount of work, he may take time out to dine on the rubbery pads of water lilies that grow in masses and lie on the pond's surface like beautifully tufted quilts. Or he may paddle over to the pond's marshy edges to feed on the sedge grass that grows there.

These water plants owe their existence to the beaver's hard labor, for they could not take root and grow but for the fact that he has provided them a wet and mucky environment. In return they offer him their flowers and roots and leaves to eat throughout spring and summer. Thus the beaver and the water plants serve each other. When any two species, be they plant and plant, animal and animal, or plant and animal, both benefit from their association with one another, they are said to have a *symbiotic* relationship.

In one respect the beaver is like man. He does not accept the world as he finds it, but reshapes it to his own liking. Many other species are able to build simple structures: foxes dig burrows, birds construct nests, even insects spin cocoons around themselves. These efforts, however, are directed toward a single end: namely, providing the animal some kind of shelter. By contrast, when a beaver settles in a new place, he alters the entire neighborhood and delays building a *lodge* in which to live until he has succeeded in putting a good deal of dry land underwater. Only the beaver and man put an entirely new face on their surroundings. But in so doing, the beaver differs from man in one important detail. The beaver transforms his environment without the aid of surveying instruments, blueprints, tools or machinery. The beaver creates his watery world with nothing but his two "hands" and chisel-like front teeth.

14

The scientific name of this wonder-worker is *Castor canadensis,* and he belongs to an order of animals called *Rodentia,* a fact that explains in part why he is able to accomplish so much. Some other familiar species in this order are the chipmunk, the squirrel, the hamster, the porcupine, the mouse and the woodchuck. All these animals have one trait in common: they are "gnawers." All possess front teeth, or *incisors,* that are especially adapted for this purpose. For example, no matter how much hard use they are subjected to, these front teeth never grow dull, for when uppers meet lowers, they automatically sharpen one another. Another unique feature of these rodent teeth is that they do not wear down to nubs as a result of constant use. The reason for this is that they never stop growing. Even as they erode on the surface, they continue to erupt at the root. This, however, can sometimes cause a problem. If an individual animal should fail to make regular and hard use of his sharp incisors, these front teeth could become so long he might find himself unable to close his mouth.

But this rarely happens. Squirrels keep their teeth filed by gnawing on hard acorns. Mice tunnel into stumps and logs and sometimes even chew their way up through the floorboards of a house. And the beaver puts his teeth to the hardest use of all. He cuts down trees with them.

At first, he works only on one side of the trunk, peeling away layer after layer of wood until he has made a deep gouge and the tree begins to groan. This is a signal that it might be ready to give way, and the beaver is keenly alert to the sound. As fast as he can move, he puts himself at a safe distance from the weakened tree. If it happens to be situated near one of his ponds, he might even dive into the water. There he will wait patiently for some time in anticipation of a crash. Beavers are sometimes killed by the timber they topple. Only those animals that are cautious survive this dangerous work.

If the tree does not fall, the beaver will return to it to tear more mouthfuls of wood from its trunk. This time he makes a fresh attack and works on the as yet uncut side of the trunk. This strategy offers him some protection, for if the tree should suddenly give way, it will naturally fall in the direction of the big notch he has already made.

Now the beaver works quickly. As he rips wood, he may glance upward at the tree's quaking crown for a sign that it is about to capsize. For when that moment arrives, there will be no one on hand to shout "Timber!" The beaver must be ready to spring to safety without any warning cry from a fellow lumberjack.

To cut a large-sized tree may take a beaver longer than a single evening. To bring down a mighty giant of a tree might even require the labor of several beavers working in shifts over several nights' time. And not infrequently all this hard labor turns out to be in vain. The tree sometimes falls against another tree and becomes "hung up." When this happens, the beavers usually accept defeat and try again elsewhere. Beavers have, however, been known to solve the problem, and in an ingenious way. By cutting and removing a section of trunk from the tree that is caught, they may cause it to drop a bit. Sometimes this is all that is needed to free its branches from those of its neighbor.

Small trees are not as likely as large ones to become entangled. Moreover, small trees can be felled quickly. It takes a beaver only a minute or so to sever a tree trunk that is two inches in diameter. *Saplings*, or very young trees, can be cut in a matter of seconds. And if a tree has produced

branches that are within a beaver's reach, he might simply clip these and leave the tree standing.

But even after a beaver has successfully toppled a large tree, his work has only begun. Next he must cut it into manageable sections and haul these to water. Once afloat, the logs and boughs can be towed to wherever they are needed. If the beaver has located a stand of favorite trees at some distance from his pond, he may even dredge a special canal to connect this "find" with his waterworks, for moving lumber on water is a lot easier than dragging it across rough ground. Thus he works hard at one task and, as a result, lightens the labor of another.

Some of the work performed by members of a beaver colony is not visible to the human eye. Only if a dam is destroyed and a pond drains does the network of underwater channels that the animals have made become apparent. These are the beavers' shipping lanes over which they float the trees they have felled. Sometimes their harvest of timber is destined to be stored beside their lodge for use as food during winter. Sometimes it has been cut for lumber and is floated to a dam in need of repair. Whatever its destination, if a bough is towed over a too shallow place, its branches become snagged on the floor of the pond. So the beavers dredge a network of channels to connect all the important places in their world. These underwater trenches serve still another important function. In winter they permit the animals to swim about under the ice, after the more shallow parts of their pond have frozen to the bottom.

And so young and old alike put in long hours of work, creating and maintaining these underwater roadways. And they perform this difficult labor using nothing but their hands. Again and again they dive to the bottom and scoop up handful after handful of muck. Sometimes a beaver will bulldoze this sediment right up onto his dam. Thus he accomplishes two tasks at once. While deepening a channel, he also raises the water

level of his pond. Then again he might swim with this material to his lodge, where he makes good use of it to plaster spaces between the support sticks of his tepee-shaped home. Thus he winterizes his living quarters. It would seem the beaver invented the idea of *recycling*, or putting waste products to good use. Even when he merely drops the dredged-up mud in one particular place in his pond, this refuse heap mounts and in time becomes an island upon which grasses take root and ducks nest.

Much of this work takes place at night, for the beaver is a *nocturnal* animal and spends most daylight hours asleep in his lodge. Some people believe, however, that *Castor canadensis* has not always been a creature of the night, for his eyes are not adapted to see in the dark. Unlike those of the big-eyed owl, their irises cannot expand much to admit what light there is. Nor do their retinas contain light-gathering crystals, as do the eyes of cats. For this reason, a beaver's eyes, like our own, do not shine in the dark when a beam of light is directed on them. One has to wonder how this species, whose night vision is likely not much better than ours, can find his way about when there is no moon.

Yet somehow he does. In early spring and late fall, he seldom emerges from his lodge much before sundown, and by sunup he has gone to bed again. To catch sight of him at these times of year, one must be observant, for he may appear but a dark shadow on the pond, a V-shaped wake that shatters the water's perfect copy of the night sky. Sometimes one can only suspect that a beaver is present when a sudden swell sets the pond in motion, causing the mirrored stars to dance.

But in summer, when nights are short, the beaver is abroad in the light, for his twelve-hour work shift demands that he get up at about the same hour every evening, regardless of how late the sun goes down. Most beavers rise sometime between five and eight o'clock and retire twelve hours later the next morning.

Nevertheless, it is a lot easier to see a beaver's works than it is to see the animal itself, for the beaver spends a good deal of time swimming underwater. He has, in fact, created his pond to escape detection and to serve as a refuge from *predators,* those animals that must kill and eat other animals to live. When moving about on land, he is slow and awkward, easy prey for bears and coyotes and mountain lions. By contrast, in the water he is swift and silent and difficult to catch. Moreover, he is able to remain submerged for almost a half hour without having to come up for air. In his own element, the beaver can outwait or outwit any animal so unwise as to pursue him, and he therefore spends a good part of his waking life in water. When he ventures onto land, he does so with caution. At the least sign of anything strange, he makes a dash for his pond.

To equip himself for this *aquatic* existence, the beaver has evolved certain features that make him appear something of an oddity. Layers of fat keep him warm even when water temperatures drop to the freezing point. The beaver's roly-poly body is not always apparent to a viewer, however, for when he is swimming on the surface, a large portion of him rides below the water level. Not until he heaves himself out of the pond and waddles up the bank does his pudgy shape become evident. An adult beaver may weigh as much as sixty pounds.

Still other adaptations indicate that the beaver has been an aquatic animal for many millions of years. Over such long ages he has had time to evolve a nose and ears that come equipped with special valves to shut out water. His eyes, too, have become well adapted to time spent below the surface. Whenever he dives, a special eyelid, through which he can see, slides over his eyeballs to protect them, like a pair of underwater goggles. (These transparent lids, when open, encircle each eye and sometimes give the animal the false appearance of being blue-eyed.) And his cheeks are so loose they can be sucked together behind his big orange teeth, allowing him to strip bark underwater without gagging. Finally, his lungs and liver have become oversized and work so efficiently that they now permit the animal to hold his breath for long periods of time without passing out or dying.

The beaver also manufactures a special "body lotion" with which he waterproofs his brown fur. This oil is secreted from two glands located on each side of his mouth. When a beaver grooms himself, he frequently touches his "fingers" to the base of his whiskers to obtain some of this oil. He then smears it on the long guard hairs that cover and protect his woolly undercoat. This done, he proceeds to comb himself with the claws of his handlike forepaws. It is of the utmost importance that the beaver tend to his coat in this way, for if his fur should become disarranged, it would lose its waterproof quality.

Usually, he begins a grooming session by cleaning his nose and his face. Next he sits up on his haunches and gives his belly a good going over (any observer who did not know what he was up to might suspect the animal had fleas!). Finally, the fastidious beaver attends to his shoulders and flanks. If he is unable to remove a piece of dirt or debris with his teeth or forepaws, he has a special tool at his disposal. Two grooming claws on each of his hind feet can be opened and closed like pairs of tweezers and, with these, he can clasp and remove any foreign matter that has become stuck in his fur. As a result of the daily care he gives his coat, a beaver's skin doesn't get wet, even though he spends most of his life in water.

In some ways the beaver looks like a kind of mythical beast put together out of a grab bag of parts taken from different animals. His front feet, which are five-fingered like those of a raccoon and which, like those of a raccoon, are able to manipulate all kinds of materials with skill, do not in any way resemble his hind feet, which are big webbed paddles similar to those of a duck.

The beaver's hairless tail is also unique. It is large, oval-shaped, flat, and leathery to the touch. It serves many purposes. When felling a tree, he uses it as a balancing prop, pushing with all his might against it as he drives his sharp teeth into the hard wood. It is also a kind of portable mattress. When grooming his fur, the animal makes himself comfortable by curling his tail under his bottom and sitting on it. When swimming,

30

this useful *appendage* may be used as a sculling oar. By wagging it from side to side, he can propel himself through the water in a sudden burst of speed. But that is not all. The beaver's all-purpose tail also allows him to communicate with others of his kind. If alarmed by the sight of a boat or a fisherman on the bank, for example, a beaver will draw his tail over his back, then suddenly bring it down on the water with a mighty thwack. The loud noise and geyserlike spray that shoots into the air alert all fellow beavers within earshot to dive for cover.

You might logically assume that the precocial baby beaver, like a baby horse or a baby bison, would be able to follow its mother about not long after birth. But beaver kits are the exception. Although they can swim perfectly well when only four days old, they are not allowed out of the lodge during their first month of life. Nor are they left alone. At night, when members of the colony swim out into the pond, one family member remains with the young to guard them. For at this stage, the babies are too buoyant to dive. Were they to fall into the water, they would not be able to get back into their house again. This is due to the unique construction of a beaver lodge. Every one of its entryways opens below the waterline so that only a diving animal is able to enter and leave the mud and stick fortress.

For this reason beavers always build their houses on water. Some rise out of the middle of a pond, like a castle protected by a moat. Others

extend out from a bank, like a peninsula, and are lapped by water on three sides only. These two styles do not differ inside. A round living chamber—perhaps three feet high and four feet in diameter—may house more than a dozen animals (depending on the number of kits born in the past two springs). This room sits high and dry above the outside surface of the pond. At a slightly lower level, a small alcove is located beside one of the *plunge* holes that lead into the water. This is the animals' lobby—a place for a wet beaver to pause and let his coat drain before climbing higher into the main chamber.

It is in the dry living chamber, safe from predators, that the beaver kits spend their first few weeks of life. Here they are nuzzled and brought food and guarded by every member of the colony. Should one fall into a plunge hole, he or she is quickly plucked out by the tail. Sometimes an attendant will even pick up a straying baby in his arms and, walking on his hind legs, tote it to safety—just as a human being carries a child. Afterward the wet youngster will be carefully groomed by an adult; for, though infant beavers begin to comb themselves when only four days old, they are not able to waterproof their own fur at first.

These are busy times for the entire family. Every day or two, while there are young in the lodge, old bedding must be pushed out into the water and fresh bedding (wood chips or grass cuttings) is collected and spread on the floor. Also, food has to be harvested and delivered to the litter. Baby beavers are born with their teeth already cut, and gnaw bark and eat leaves when only a few days old.

At one month the litter is ready to make a first excursion into the pond, and the event is well attended by the family. A supervisor, in fact, swims alongside them, so as to allow any kit who tires to ride piggyback. Back and forth between lodge and shore they swim. At this age the youngsters quickly master the art of diving and, in a night or two, are allowed to enter and leave the lodge when they please. Accustomed as they are to the constant company of others, however, they tend to tag after the older beavers, who no doubt serve as role models for them.

Imitating others is one way an animal can learn. And baby beavers must acquire many skills in the two years before they set off on their own to create a whole new world of water. Although they are certainly born with a kind of building know-how coded in their brains, they nevertheless must organize and perfect these *innate* abilities. To do so requires time and practice. Like human babies, they handle objects awkwardly at first. By contrast, adult beavers possess unusual *dexterity*, meaning they are skilled in the use of their hands. For example, they are able to aim and wedge a stick or a stone into a tiny hole in their dam with absolute precision. They also roll lily pads into manageable shapes before inserting them into their mouths. By contrast, kits grab the big floppy leaves haphazardly and try to eat around the edges. As a result, they sometimes end up wearing their food on their heads. Yet, after a period of face-to-face feeding with an adult, the youngsters, too, begin to roll the rubbery pads.

40

Observing others would seem, however, to be about the only labor the young-of-the-year perform during their first spring and summer. Although they sometimes make digging and building motions in thin air, they do not add a single stick to the dam, nor do they dredge mud from the pond bottom. And when the adults fell a tree, the youngsters simply wait in the water and whimper until some branches have been cut and dragged within their reach.

They are relentless wheedlers. Any adult or yearling who makes the mistake of eating within the presence of a kit must constantly jerk his food out of reach of the imploring youngster. Sometimes there is nothing for an adult to do but relent and share the very branch upon which he or she is feeding with a whining baby.

42

Because wood contains no food value, it is not eaten by beavers. They consume bark, the underside of which is lined with a nutritious substance called *cambium* (the same foodstuff that keeps the tree alive). To separate the edible bark from the wood, a beaver grasps a branch with his two hands and slowly rotates it, while gnawing at a furious rate—just as a hungry human being eats corn on the cob. Afterward he may drop the pared stick on the ground or leave it floating in the pond. This beaver *sign* is unmistakable evidence that the species is present in the area. If you examine the stick you will see neat rows of tooth marks etched in the wood.

Not until fall do the kits lend a hand in any of the colony's work projects. Their first task is to help store food for winter. This effort begins in late October or early November, and all members of the family take part. First, the adults and yearlings dredge a hole in the floor of the pond near the lodge. This hole must be of sufficient size to contain all the branches the beavers will gather. Next the adults and yearlings begin to cut trees in earnest. At this time of year, no tree is so large as to discourage a beaver from attacking it. And once felled, even gigantic trees are cut into sections and transported to the hole in short order. There, one by

one, each bough and branch is driven into the mucky bottom, butt end first. Every beaver helps in the towing and planting. Clutching a branch in his teeth, a small kit may have to attempt several dives before he finally succeeds in sinking his contribution into the floor of the pond, for wood tends to bob to the surface and float. In time, however, the growing *food raft* becomes a mesh of intertwining twigs into which additional branches can be inserted with ease.

Invariably, beavers cut poplar and willow and birch before they show any interest in toppling harder woods such as oak and maple. Evergreen trees are rarely used. Not until a colony has inhabited a pond for many years and has exhausted much of its food supply does it begin to harvest these less desirable trees. Aspen, a member of the poplar family, is the beaver's favorite food. Fortunately, this family of trees has evolved two ways to reproduce and so can withstand heavy use. Besides dropping seeds, poplars send up new shoots from old roots—a system of reproduction called *cloning*. Even after one of these species has been cut and carried off by a beaver, a new tree will grow out of its root system.

46

Winter is a perilous time for wild animals; many die of hunger and cold. To cope, every species has devised some kind of strategy. Many birds *migrate,* or fly to warmer climates. Voles create a world of tunnels between the snow pack and the ground. Snowshoe hares and weasels disguise themselves by turning white. Some animals—bears and woodchucks and bats—*hibernate,* or pass the winter in a profound state of sleep. The beaver, however, neither slumbers nor moves south. His life goes on as usual except for one important detail. He spends the season under a roof of ice. For when his pond freezes, he can no longer go ashore. He cannot even poke his head up out of the water to take a deep breath. He can of course swim in and out of his lodge, for, as we know, the entryways to that amazing structure open underwater.

47

Perhaps old beavers are able to recollect past winters and so try to delay their dark imprisonment for as long as possible. Whatever their reason, they make systematic efforts to keep their ponds from freezing. When temperatures drop and a thin layer of ice begins to form on their waterways, they punch through it from below. Then they rise to the surface and, with their forepaws, push down on the edges of the opening, breaking off huge slabs.

And who can blame them? Imagine yourself a member of a beaver colony, sealed off by snow and ice in a dark and crowded chamber. Every time you want to eat, you must dive into the icy water and swim to the family food larder. Perhaps, to enjoy a few minutes of solitude, you may choose to remain underwater while you feed on a branch. Given your special adaptations, you will have no trouble doing this. Or you may simply detach a piece of poplar or willow or birch from the food raft and return with it to the lodge. There you can breathe and drain and eat all at once. Back inside, however, you may have difficulty reclaiming a place for yourself amid the crowd of damp beavers. Moreover, you must do this in complete darkness, for no light can penetrate the thickly plastered walls of a beaver lodge. For that matter, very little air seeps in through the small, uncovered *venthole* at the top.

It is hard to understand how, under such stressful conditions, a family of beavers manages to get along together. Many species would not. Rats become vicious when crowded. If a family of wolves or a pride of lions were forced to live in such close quarters, they would surely get into a row over food. Even people begin to behave strangely after a prolonged period of confinement. They are then said to be suffering from "cabin fever."

But the vegetarian beaver is a peaceable animal, and he has evolved a number of social strategies for maintaining good relations with his kin. For example, while passing time, the animals frequently groom one another, a soothing and pleasurable activity that helps cement family bonds. Also, older beavers are often helpful to younger ones. Yearlings will even enter the cold water to bring back branches for the already half-grown kits to eat. What's more, the family members "talk." What they have to say to one another can be known only to themselves, but on certain winter days, their lilting murmurs can be heard even through the thick walls of their snow-domed home. Anyone who has stood beside a beaver lodge in winter and listened to the animals "converse"—in tones not unlike those used by contented human beings—can be forgiven for imagining that there are tiny folk inside. Small wonder that certain tribes of North American Indians viewed beavers as "little Indians" and sometimes even made pets of them.

And so the gentle beaver bears up over winter. He even invents ways to expand his icebound horizons. For example, by gnawing a hole near the top of his dam, he releases water and lowers the level of his pond. This creates a layer of air between the pond's surface and its ice cover. As a result, the beaver extends the time he can swim about under the ice. When the moment arrives that he must take a breath, he need not hurry back to his lodge. Instead, he pokes his nose into this sandwich of air and inhales.

Then, as winter wears on, he might enlarge this *spillway* just enough so that he can slip through it and so break out of his ice prison. Once ashore,

perhaps he will cut a small tree and feed on it. Or maybe he will drag the cutting back through the escape hatch he has created and add it to the family food raft. One thing is certain, however: if the temperature of the outside air is below freezing, he will stay out only a short time. A wet beaver might not survive long in air that is colder than the freezing point of water. His underwater world, however frigid it may feel, can never be *that* cold or it would turn to solid ice. Also, a danger exists that in his absence the spillway, through which he made his departure, might freeze again and lock him out of his pond.

And so the beaver returns to his world of ice and water, and as he travels home to his lodge, a trail of small bubbles escapes from his fur and marks his route. And a few larger bubbles are expelled from his lungs. These bubbles can be seen through the ice, clinging to it, like tiny helium balloons whose ascent to the skies has been stopped by a ceiling. And when you see this beaver sign, you know the animal is present. But you will probably have to wait until spring to see him.

Anyone who has watched beavers cavorting about a pond in late March has to wonder if the animals might not be rejoicing in their recently recovered freedom. Or is it spring they are celebrating? Do beavers notice when willow trees begin to leaf? Or are they simply releasing pent-up energy after having been housebound for so long? Young and old alike plunge and surface, plunge and surface, plunge and surface. Sometimes one beaver will porpoise over the body of another, as the two swim back and forth across the pond. Sometimes a beaver will even roll over on his back and float, like an otter. The colony never appears to be in such high spirits. The beavers never seem so engaging.

But soon the family will break up. Last year's kits are nearly one year old now. They will stay at home for yet another year. Last year's *yearlings* are almost two years old now. In another month they will feel an irresistible urge to seek their fortunes elsewhere. For soon new kits will be born to the founding pair, who in February mated under the ice.

Meanwhile there is work to be done. Before long two-year-olds from everywhere will be on the move, seeking suitable habitat in which to settle. Each colony must therefore *post* its property to inform these young *emigrants* to pass on through. An unrelated animal is not welcome on a colony's *territory,* and for a very practical reason. There would not be food and space enough to support every beaver who would surely find a family's readymade waterworks an inviting place to settle. Only if one of the founding pair should die, will an outsider—a new mate—be allowed to join the colony. All other beavers must keep out. To alert them to this fact, "no trespassing" signs are placed at conspicuous locations throughout the property. Beavers of both sexes create these notices.

The beaver begins with bottom muck, which he digs out of the pond with his hands. He may simply shove this debris up on the bank, where he will then treat it chemically. Or, should he wish to deposit it farther inland, he will rise on his hind legs and, walking *bipedally,* carry it on outstretched "arms" to the place he has in mind. Once he has plopped it onto a stone or atop a small rise, he will spray it with substances secreted from two pair of glands. These glands are located in a special pouch, called a *cloaca,* on his lower abdomen.

To do this, he must position his body over the mud mound so that his cloaca is in line with it. Next he douses it with oil manufactured in his anal glands. The scent of this oil reveals a great deal of information that can be read by another beaver's nose. It may for example disclose the beaver's sex, whether or not the animal is mature, what he has been eating lately and the state of his health. But the mound-maker is not finished yet. He must also spray the mud with *castoreum,* a substance manufactured in his castor glands. Scientists now believe that castoreum is simply a fixative used to prolong the effectiveness of the oil deposited by the beaver's anal glands.

53

Frequently, after one beaver has created a *scent mound*, others in the colony add their spray to it. A wandering beaver who sniffs such a concoction of odors knows at once that a number of animals inhabit the area. He will not try to contest their claim, for he would surely be overwhelmed. Instead, he quickly passes through the area and so avoids doing battle.

Species that possess sharp teeth with which to obtain food for themselves must avoid using these hazardous tools against their own kind. Consider how dangerous the beaver could be in combat. With his razor-sharp incisors, he is able to sever large trees. Should he sink these into the hide of another beaver, more than likely he would kill him. On occasion, full-scale fights do occur, and they are bloody affairs. But it is not in the best interest of the beaver to kill its own kind. A species that would make it a practice to do so would in time become extinct. The beaver, therefore, has evolved strategies by which he avoids conflict. Making scent mounds is one of them.

54

Meanwhile, two-year-old beavers must find suitable places in which to live. A lake or a stretch of river would of course be most desirable. But these natural waterways are not likely to be unoccupied. Most young beavers have to be satisfied with something that is less ideal—perhaps a tract of wooded land fed by a brook. The brook need not carry much water; a mere trickle will do. By applying his engineering skills, the beaver will be able to dam its flow and so create a large pond.

But though he may follow a stream for a great distance in search of such modest requirements, and though he may even travel overland to investigate distant *watersheds,* or drainage systems, a young beaver may experience great difficulty finding any place at all to live. Most watered property is already occupied—either by other beavers or by man. And while property-holding beavers do, at least, put out notices to inform any aspiring homesteader of their prior claim, man does not. As a result, many two-year-old animals try to create ponds from farmers' irrigation ditches, and as a result turn planted fields into swamps. They also dam up culverts and put country roads under water. And man has little patience with wild animals that interfere with his projects. More than likely, such a mischief-maker will be trapped and killed. At the very least, the animal's works will be torn apart—a setback that will greatly reduce his chances for survival. For a two-year-old beaver is on a tight schedule. Before winter arrives, he must have completed a great deal of work. His dams must be built, his pond must be deep, his channels must be dredged, his lodge must be finished and he must have cut and stored enough wood to last

him for three months. It is not surprising that most young beavers do not survive their first year away from home. What is surprising is that these fully grown animals are sometimes allowed to return to their family pond. Even after an absence of several years, they are recognized as kin and accepted back into the family fold.

But two-year-old beavers are not the only ones who suffer at the hand of man. Many women (and some men now, too) regard it a sign of fashion to wear beaver fur. To supply this market, trappers place *drown-sets* underwater near beaver lodges. These devices snap shut on the animal's foot and hold him fast until he dies for want of air. It takes a beaver more than half an hour to drown, during which time the panicked victim may try to escape by wringing off the foot that is caught. Crippled beavers, if they survive, have a difficult time in life.

Still, some people feel it is an American tradition to trap beavers. Certainly, the quest for this animal's fur played a part in the exploration and history of our land. The story, however, is not one in which all Americans take pride. In fact, the greedy scramble for beaver skins nearly brought the species to extinction.

As early as the 17th Century, Dutch settlers were using the beaver's pelt in place of money, for at the time, the animal's fur was greatly in demand in Europe. No well-dressed gentleman considered himself properly attired without a beaver top hat. Because this fashion craze had already brought the European beaver to the brink of extinction, hat makers abroad were forced to look to the New World for a source of fur. And trappers here were only too happy to supply this market. They went after the beaver with a vengeance. When a horde of trappers brought a surplus of pelts to the fur market, thousands of the skins were burned just to keep the price of beaver fur from falling. It didn't take long before the animal began to grow scarce here too.

To trap out an entire colony was easy. The beaver's lodge, which had over long ages served to protect its makers from their natural enemies, now simply alerted the fur hunters to the species' whereabouts. Not until every beaver had been captured from a particular pond would traps be removed and set in a new location. When no more animals were left in the East, the pelt seekers traveled westward, leaving a trail of beaver ghost towns in their wake. By 1800 so few beavers could be found within the borders of what was then the United States that John Jacob Astor sent an expedition across Indian Territory into Oregon Country to hunt the animal there. Not many years passed before that region, too, was emptied of beavers. By the end of the 19th Century, every state in the union declared the animal to be either entirely gone or nearly so.

Fortunately, for *Castor canadensis*, just when extinction seemed inevitable, some early *conservationists* made efforts to help the species. First they persuaded their various state legislatures to pass bills making it illegal to trap the animal. Then they imported beaver pairs from those few places where the species could still be found. Luckily, the transplanted animals thrived in their new surroundings. As a result, numbers began to grow. Today the beaver is found in every one of our states except Hawaii and is no longer endangered.

Nevertheless, even though the beaver has made an impressive recovery, it is still not free from persecution. Many people view it as a pest, one that chews down ornamental trees and floods golf courses. Still others measure its worth only by the going price on its pelt. They seem unaware of the extraordinary benefits beavers provide not only to other animals, but to man. For, thanks to the beaver's industrious efforts to stop water flow, pools are formed, melting snow is conserved and underground water tables are raised. We as a nation are only now beginning to face the problems of dwindling water supplies. To answer our future needs, many farsighted people are already looking to the beaver for help. For example, in a dry and treeless part of Wyoming, biologists recently provided a pair of struggling beavers with a load of old tires in the hope that the animals would use the artificial building material to create dams and store badly needed water. The strategy worked. In one year's time, the area had been transformed. Willow trees and other water-loving plants were sprouting. Elsewhere, too, beavers are helping man restore lands that have been overused and abused.

Equally important to man is the beaver's service as a soil saver. Sediment is constantly being washed off the ground and carried seaward by streams and rivers. But where beavers have constructed dams, water flow is slowed, and as a result, suspended particles of earth settle to the bottom. In time, a beaver's quiet pool becomes so clogged with this rich *silt* that its inhabitants are forced to relocate. What was once a pond then becomes a luxuriant meadow—a rich field that supports an entirely new array of animals. Rabbits and voles and deer flourish. And, in turn, these species feed bobcats and owls and foxes. But it doesn't end there. When man seeks a place to grow crops or to graze livestock or to plant orchards, he can find no richer, more suitable land than that which was created by beavers.

That a beady-eyed, sausage-shaped rodent can accomplish all this is surely cause for wonder. His intricate waterworks, created in the dark of night, would as likely seem the doing of a magician. For, when the light of morning shines on his handiwork, the beaver is nowhere to be seen.

He has retired to his lodge for a well-earned rest. Unlike man, he feels no need to cruise about his pond admiring all his latest improvements. Nor does he require thanks from all the wild creatures for whom he has provided a home. The beaver works solely for himself and is unaware that his labor is of any importance to others. Still, it seems only fitting that we acknowledge and salute his valuable services. He is, after all, our first and our foremost conservationist.

Index